A+ books

3-D Shapes

Cylinders

by Nathan Olson

Capstone press

Mankato, Minnesota

A+ Books are published by Capstone Press,
151 Good Counsel Drive, P.O. Box 669, Mankato, Minnesota 56002.
www.capstonepress.com

1 2 3 4 5 6 12 11 10 09 08 07

Library of Congress Cataloging-in-Publication Data
Olson, Nathan.
    Cylinders / by Nathan Olson.
    p. cm.—(A+ books. 3-D shapes)
    Summary: "Simple text and color photographs introduce cylinder shapes and give examples of cylinders in
the real world"—Provided by publisher.
    Includes bibliographical references and index.
    ISBN-13: 978-1-4296-0050-7 (hardcover)
    ISBN-10: 1-4296-0050-0 (hardcover)
    1. Cylinder (Mathematics)—Juvenile literature. 2. Shapes—Juvenile literature. 3. Geometry, Solid—Juvenile
literature. I. Title. II. Series.
QA491.O445 2008
516'.154—dc22   2006037421

Credits

Jenny Marks, editor; Alison Thiele, designer; Scott Thoms and Charlene Deyle, photo researchers;
    Kelly Garvin, photo stylist

Photo Credits

Capstone Press/Alison Thiele, cover (illustrations), 7 (illustration), 29 (illustrations); Karon Dubke, 4, 5,
    6, 8–9, 10, 11, 12–13, 14, 19, 20–21, 22, 23, 24–25, 29 (craft)
Fotolia/marilyna, 15
Getty Images Inc./Tim Graham, 26
iStockphoto/slobo mitic, 27
Peter Arnold/Jorgen Schytte, 16–17
Shutterstock/Cathleen Clapper, 18

Note to Parents, Teachers, and Librarians

This 3–D Shapes book uses full color photographs and a nonfiction format to introduce the concept
of cylinder shapes. *Cylinders* is designed to be read aloud to a pre-reader or to be read independently
by an early reader. Photographs help listeners and early readers understand the text and concepts
discussed. The book encourages further learning by including the following sections: Table of
Contents, It's a Fact, Hands On, Glossary, Read More, Internet Sites, and Index. Early readers may
need assistance using these features.

Table of Contents

What Are 3-D Shapes? 4

Cylinders at Home 8

Cylinders at Work.............. 16

All Sorts of Cylinders...........20

It's a Fact............................26

Hands On 28

Glossary 30

Read More 31

Internet Sites 31

Index 32

What Are 3-D Shapes?

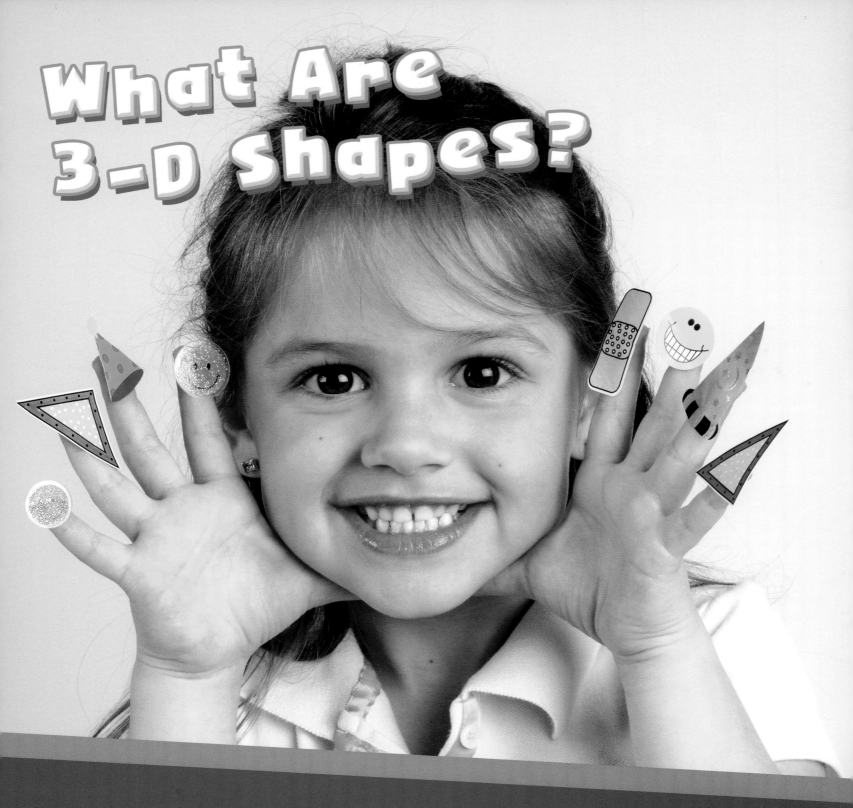

Flat shapes on stickers are easy to see! These two-dimensional, or 2-D, shapes have height and width, but no depth.

These beads are 3-D shapes.
Three-dimensional shapes have
height, width, and depth.

A cylinder is a 3–D shape with two circle–shaped bases. The middle of a cylinder is one smooth, curved surface.

base

Two identical circles and one rectangle make the cylinder's net.

Cylinders at Home

A long, thin cylinder rolls colorful play dough smooth and flat.

Some cylinders flip their lids
to hold what you throw away.

Pantry shelves hold cylinders full of food.

Batteries are cylinder-shaped
power packs that make toys go!

13

Rat-a-tat-tat! Toy drums are cylinders you can tap, rap, and beat.

Other cylinders hold nuts and seeds
that feathered friends love to eat.

Cylinders at Work

The big, powerful cylinder on a steamroller presses roadways smooth.

Utility poles are tall cylinders that reach high in the sky. They hold wires for telephones and electricity.

Painters change plain walls into colorful ones with a cylinder called a paint roller.

19

All Sorts of Cylinders

Abracadabra! A magician's wand is shaped like a cylinder. A tall magic hat looks like a cylinder too.

Hair wrapped around cylinders becomes a bunch of bouncy curls.

Checkers is a game played with short black and red cylinders.

Glowing cylinders on your birthday cake show how old you are. Make a wish!

24

It's a Fact

Can you find a cylinder in your kitchen? Soup cans are almost always shaped like cylinders. The Campbell's soup can label is red and white. In 1900, Campbell's soups won a gold medal at the Paris Exposition in France. A picture of that medal appears on almost every can.

Think you could toss a telephone pole? A traditional Scottish game called the caber toss involves throwing what looks like a small utility pole. Players hold up the cylinder and toss it end over end.

Thread comes wound on cylinders called spools. Spools were once made of wood, but today they are almost always plastic.

A huge cylinder in Malaysia is one of the tallest concrete towers in the world. It is made with more than 30 tons (27 metric tons) of concrete. That's about the same weight as 10 adult elephants!

Cylinder–shaped columns called pillars appear on many government buildings. How many cylinders do you see on the California State Capitol building?

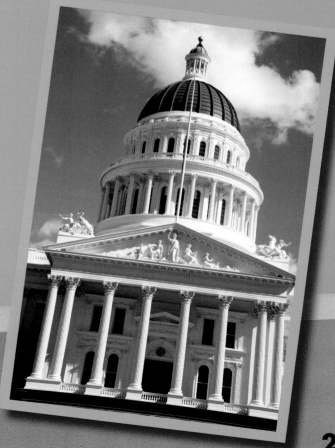

Hands On
Cindy the Cylinder

You can decorate a 3-D shape to make a friend named Cindy the Cylinder.

What You Need

- [ ] cylinder-shaped box or canister
- [ ] scissors
- [ ] glue or tape
- [ ] construction paper
- [ ] decorations (buttons, pipe cleaners, felt, googly eyes, yarn)

What You Do

1 Glue or tape a strip of construction paper around the cylinder.

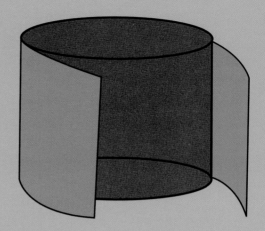

2 Glue decorations on the cylinder to make a funny face for Cindy.

Glossary

base (BAYSS)—a flat side that a 3-D shape can stand on

depth (DEPTH)—how deep something is

height (HITE)—how tall something is

identical (eye-DEN-ti-kuhl)—exactly alike

three-dimensional (THREE-duh-MEN-shun-uhl)—having length, width, and height; three-dimensional is often shortened to 3-D.

two-dimensional (TOO-duh-MEN-shun-uhl)—having height and width; flat; two-dimensional is often shortened to 2-D.

utility pole (yoo-TIL-uh-tee POHL)—a tall, smooth cylinder made of wood, metal, or plastic that is used to hold wires that carry electricity

width (WIDTH)—how wide something is

Read More

Kompelien, Tracy. *3–D Shapes Are Like Green Grapes!* Math Made Fun. Edina, Minn.: Abdo, 2007.

Shepard, Daniel. *Solid Shapes.* Yellow Umbrella Books for Early Readers. Bloomington, Minn.: Yellow Umbrella Books, 2006.

Internet Sites

FactHound offers a safe, fun way to find Internet sites related to this book. All of the sites on FactHound have been researched by our staff.

Here's how:

1. Visit *www.facthound.com*
2. Choose your grade level.
3. Type in this book ID **1429600500** for age-appropriate sites. You may also browse subjects by clicking on letters, or by clicking on pictures and words.
4. Click on the **Fetch It** button.

FactHound will fetch the best sites for you!

Index

2-D shapes, 4

3-D shapes, 5, 6

bases, 6

buildings, 27

cans, 11, 26

checkers, 23

circles, 6, 7

cylinder net, 7

depth, 4, 5,

height, 4, 5

poles, 18, 26

rectangles, 7

width, 4, 5